I0428672

Intro:

Icebreaker: What do you know about Culture.
What do you think of when you hear the word "Culture?"

(Activity)
CAfW: What is it?

CAFW, Cultural Anthropology for Writers, is an attempt to help some writers with world-building, (also called Conworlding) by forcing them to think about their fictional worlds as cultures and writing the interactions from that point of view.

 The reason behind this is simple, culture is what makes us say that something is 'out of character' for a fictional entity, and it also allows the writer to use the culture of the city or world as a character itself. But even if they don't it allows a writer to know enough about the culture to be able to write it consistently without breaking the rules they set down at the beginning.

 What I am attempting to do is prevent some of the big world-building mistakes that our readers, and fellow writers will notice. Firstly, let's go over a few world-building mistakes.

The first one I have named after the screenwriter most notorious for it, a "Lucas" is a total lack of cultural development to the point that a character can be uprooted from their home and thrown in with others from any other point in the galaxy and there is not a single cultural snafu.

For instance, Luke, Leia and Solo in the Falcon with Chewie, four different cultures and other than the remark about letting the wookie win, there is no cultural difference between them, and yet, it is clear that Solo is from a place where law is a matter of opinion and power, where pirates and thieves are revered (as shown by his attitude.) but never once are we given any hint of where he is from. And, with Leia, The Senator's daughter from Alderaan, who, when confronted with the destruction of her world said, "we have no weapons of war," and yet is surprisingly comfortable and proficient with a blaster. Not so much as a "it wasn't always this easy." He gives us flat characters and non-existent culture as a basis of reality.

Our second big mistake is to assume that everyone knows culture, and that all cultures are the same. Now, unless you are in an alternate universe where all but a few of the laws are exactly the same, you will have to do some Conworlding, and even then Cultural expectations differ from nation to nation, and, you will have to find a way to bring that world Construction into the story or it will not work.

What are some other examples of film, book and television world construction/culture construction issues you can think of?

What is culture?

Culture is more than a name and a place. It is more than the language we speak. What are some unique Cultural expression and expectations of being here in America?

Who or what is "uncle Sam?

Complete the phrase "_____ Liberty" Or "Blind _____"

According to the dictionary Culture is:

> *The integrated pattern of human knowledge, belief, and behavior that depends upon the capacity for learning and transmitting knowledge to succeeding generations*
>
> *The customary beliefs, social forms, and material traits of a racial, religious, or social group*
>
> *The characteristic features of everyday existence (as diversions or a way of life} shared by people in a place or time*
>
> *The set of shared attitudes, values, goals, and practices that characterizes an institution or organization*
>
> *The set of values, conventions, or social practices associated with a particular field, activity, or societal norm*

(Resource center Online. "Definition of Culture" "http://aim.search.aol.com/aol/search?&query=Culture%2C+Definition+of&invocation Type=tb50-ff-aim-ab-en-us) Truncated definition 5)

In short, it can be said that Culture is: the shared belief systems affecting how a group sees, relates to, and interacts with their surroundings.

It is also defined as:
> ***Culture:*** *is a shared, learned, symbolic system of values, beliefs and attitudes that shapes and influences perception and behavior -- an abstract "mental blueprint" or "mental code."*
>
> *Must be studied "indirectly" by studying behavior, customs, material culture (artifacts, tools, technology), language, etc.*
>
> * ***Learned.*** *Process of learning one's culture is called* underlying{enculturation.}
> * ***Shared*** *by the members of a society. No "culture of one."*
> * ***Patterned.*** *People in a society live and think in ways that form definite patterns.*
> * ***Mutually constructed*** *through a constant process of social interaction.*

- ***Symbolic****. Culture, language and thought are based on symbols and symbolic meanings.*
- ***Arbitrary.*** *Not based on "natural laws" external to humans, but created by humans according to the "whims" of the society. Example: standards of beauty.*
- ***Internalized.*** *Habitual.   Taken-for-granted.   Perceived as "natural."*

(Http://www2.eou.edu/~kdahl/cultdef.html)

That's a pretty broad definition, which is why so many people fail to use it. They don't want to deal with the belief systems that define their world. For instance, the only outlined culture in Star wars is actually the Jedi, and that isn't even until you get to the training with the Padawan learners. They have a caste system and a set of mantras and beliefs that affect how they interact with the world and how they view themselves and each other in relation to those laws. A 'dark Jedi' or Sith is one who has transgressed the belief systems of the Jedi and have therefore, become a sub or counter-culture movement of the Jedi.

All true societies have culture and counter-culture. A counter-culture is simply a sub culture that has placed itself against the main beliefs of the primary culture of the world/ race or belief.

Religion: While this is not overtly a class on religion, it may be necessary to use religion in your stories. Religion can be a very powerful motivation and most wars have started over religious views or politics. Therefore, religion cannot be dismissed lightly. For those of you who may be from any other belief system, or the belief of non-religion, what you believe, what your characters believe can change how they look at things. Religious leanings in characters can fuel changes both for the good and for the bad.

It is not my intention to allow this class to degenerate into a religious or political free-for all, so I ask that whatever your views are, whatever your characters views are, that you show respect to practitioners of any and all faiths, for the purpose of the class, I will be digging into religion a little, so please be respectful to those in the class.
**

While many say that religion is not absolutely necessary, it can often color culture and counter-culture, so for the purposes of this work it is included as a category, the decision of religious or Athiest will change the world-view of the culture significantly.

In order to be able to build a culture, we must first understand how you study a culture. Because of our definition of Culture, you must study the systems of responses, and taboos and mores before you can actually understand a culture.

Why is this important?

Well, besides the fact that it is on the test, culture is important to world building because without culture, we end up with flat characters and un-interesting worlds. Culture is one of the major supports for the Suspension bridge of Disbelief. Without it, it is much harder for the reader to throw themselves into the story.

Your first assignment is to use the Foundations of Culture worksheet provided in the packet (I do have copies, but since we may use more than one copy, I recommend copying it before you write on it, or downloading it from my site.)

Fill in the worksheet for whatever Culture you are currently working on in your stories. Now, a word about the worksheet, you notice it is a single, one-sided sheet, I've done that on purpose, this is just a place to start. Please just give me the broad strokes, this is just a brain-teaser to get you thinking. Any extra information should be on paper labled with the correct heading, you may need it later.

Welcome to Foundations. The first section in Cultural Anthropology for Writers. Here we will learn some of the basics of the world and city we are creating. All work here is proprietary to the author.

First, stop and download the Foundations Worksheet and fill it out. We will be going over many of the sections in detail. This worksheet is meant to be a guide for at-a glance Culture questions about language, area, military, government and everyday life questions. It is not all inclusive and you will notice that it is not set up for long answers, this is really just meant to get you thinking and to give you a starting point. Any excess information should be put in margins, on the back or on a separate piece of paper.

Name:

General Topography:

General Geography:

Magic:
Yes ___ No ___
Type:
Practitioner:

Religion:
State: Yes ___ No ___
Correlation to magic?
Yes ___ No ___
Antagonistic to Magic?
Yes ___ No ___
Practitioners:
Preists:

Education:
State Sponsored? Yes ___ No ___
Universal? Yes ___ No ___
Is there a Written Language?
Yes ___ No ___
If yes, What type?
Alphabetic _____ Runic ___
Heiroglyphic ___ Other ___

Housing and Status
Housing:
Owned ___
Rented ___
Other ___
Does Land ownership equate to status?
Yes ___ No ___
Do they own:
Personal Property: ___
Land: ___
Slaves: ___
Other: ___

General timeline

General Tech Level:
Pre history   Post apocalyptic
Pre industry   Post nuclear
Pre-flight   Post space
Pre-gunpowder Post flight
           Other

Perceieved world:

Government.
Type:
Ruled by:
Market type:
Currency: Yes ___ no ___
If yes:
What is it called?
Is it used everywhere?
What is most common denomination?

Least?

How is it measured?
Is it used for religious purposes?
Yes ___ No ___
Is there a Class System? Yes:__ No:__
If yes;
How is it divided?
What is your MC's social class?

Language:
Primary:
Spoken by:
Secondary:
Spoken by:
How is it divided?
Class___ Social Status___ Race ___
Which does your MC speak?

Introduction

Foundation: Underpinning or basis.

Just as a building has to have a solid foundation, so too does a story world have to have a proper foundation in order to handle the rigors of plot and contrivance. Whether your world is Urban adventure, far future Sci-fi or mythic fantasy, they must all have not just a story, but a world.

Before we get started with the actual world building we have to know what our foundation is. Foundation is a series of pillars that if any one is missing, the suspension bridge that allows you to suspend your disbelief comes crashing down.

The backbone of the world is Culture, and that is because Cultural Identification is what sets us apart. Culture is the root of most wars and most genocides too.

Foundation of culture isn't simply giving it a name it means time, technology, language, religious expectation, money, education and many other things.

Please turn to the Foundations of Culture worksheet, or, if you are on the website, please download and complete it before you continue.

I'll wait...

Ok, all done?... No? ... Yes?

I mean you in the back too. You need to finish, not because I tell you to but because it is important as a road map for future sections.

 So many people create a new world by putting letters on a page, in an order, calling it a name, and saying they have a new world with its own culture. No, what you have with a name, is a start. Even the physical information of geography, and galactography is only a start. Because the thing that makes many of the best stories great is that they are not just places with the rules we know. They have actually built customs and taboos into the world, they have given it history, language and culture.

 Look at Tolkein. Each of his races didn't have just a language, but also a culture. They had things they expected, things they did, things they believed. The things that make us 'family' are the things that make our culture unique. Over the course of this class, I hope to give you some ability to be able to create not just empty languages and stick figure people, but fully-fleshed cultures that will keep you from having to explain yourself later.

The first thing you need to is stop and fill out the "Foundation of Culture' worksheet. This is the biographical data about the physical place, and the overarching type of story you are telling. A culture with a dictatorship is going to be different than a democratic culture.

If you come to a question on the Foundations worksheet and you haven't yet answered the question yourself, mark it and go on. Come back to it later. The foundations worksheet is brief, it is not meant for a treatise on magic or a history of the language. Instead, it is to get you thinking about all the things that people forget to ask. I don't give much space, and much of it is merely yes/no. That is intentional. The foundations is just to give us a starting point and to paint your world in broad strokes.

You want to use general and broad terms during this part because when we get to the signal systems in Part Two, your answers may change. The worksheet is also for an at-a-glance reference. That way you always spell things correctly, you always know what the general education level is or that the neighbors to the north are unfriendly. You never know when these foundational things can come in handy as back story and sub-plot.

Most writers simply put a name on a page. You can call a place Dwaarat. But understanding why it is called Dwaaarat and what that means to the people who live there will serve the story better.

(Cultural significance slide show.)
Foundations overview

Like a play or a movie, what happens in a novel and the very genre of the book can depend on the setting. The setting not only tells the reader where and or when they are, but also what sort of world they are in. Unfortunately, many novelists overlook this silent, but very important character. And just like most forgotten characters this one can help or hinder your character's goals, help you reflect a mood, or give you a chance to foreshadow a decision or plot point later in the novel.

The questions on the foundations worksheet are a starting point. The questions are simply meant to get you thinking about your world in terms of not only what it is but how it interacts with your characters, and how they interact with it. Don't panic if your answers change as you go deeper on, it just means that you understand more about how your society works and why your people act the way they do.

We will be using your foundations of Culture worksheet as a guide, but it is a loose guide. It might help you to keep a clean copy nearby in case you want to change your answers to something else. DO NOT THROW AWAY OLD COPIES. I have learned this mistake the hard way. You never know when that one will be part of something else.

Also, keep a piece of scratch paper handy to write down any notes or ideas that you may get from this lecture.

Foundations overview-

If you, as a writer, break too many of the pillars by not doing your homework and grounding them in backstory, then the whole suspension bridge itself will come crashing down and your reader will walk away without finishing the story. What you need to do is build up the supports that will allow your reader to suspend the disbelief without any trouble.

Since you have filled out the Foundations worksheet, let's go back to that. For the sake of organization I have split it up into two sections, roughly geopolitical and geographic.

Section One: in depth, nation, city state,

What do you call it? Or "You live WHERE?"
My first question is always name, mainly because I like knowing where we are and where we are going.

The best place to start with a new world or country is with a name. Even if it is on another world, focus first on the culture of the city your MC inhabits. This way you can see what is going on around him/her that will affect the way he or she sees the world. So, give me the name of the place. And try to use a name that gives you a 'flavor' of the world. It doesn't do to have a place named LJLGJL if you don't tell us how to say it or why it is named that way. It also doesn't do to have a name Shambala for a place that doesn't believe in magic unless you give us a compelling reason why. The name is the first thing most of your readers will ever know, and it is the first pillar that holds up the suspension of disbelief.

If you, as a writer, break too many of the pillars by not doing your homework and grounding them in backstory, then the whole suspension bridge itself will come crashing down and your reader will walk away without finishing the story. What you need to do is build up the supports that will allow your reader to suspend the disbelief without any trouble.

Since you have filled out the Foundations worksheet, let's go back to that. What is the name of your world? How do you spell that? (Check your spelling. You wouldn't want to find out later that you have been spelling it wrong.) What is the name of your MC's town? Is it the capital? Is it large? Is it small? Will any of the story take place there? If so, complete the rest of the exercise for the home town, if not, complete it for the town in which your MC will be interacting. But keep the information handy for any other towns you may use.

Section one, Geography, Topography, magic, era and science

Geography and Politics

So, the Name of your world? (check your spelling.)

If a planet other than Earth, What system are we in?

How do you say it? (Write your phonetic pronunciation so that you remember)

What is the name of your MC's birth Country?

Your Setting Country?

Name of your State/municipality?

Name of the region or county?

Was your MC born in the Capital?

Was your MC born in the city in which your story is set?
 If not:
How far away is it?

Name of the current city, and relationship to capital, and/or MC's city of birth.

How is it politically aligned? (Does alignment depend on outside factors such as class, gender, religion, magic, race or age?)

Does it share the same alignment as the MC's city?

Is this city/state/region known for anything in particular? (Is it the only place to get a certain food or mineral? Is it the only place to train for a certain trade? Is it the only place to train mages? Any of these can be plot points later. Not just good stuff, are they known for rebels? Do they have a plague?

Politics

The name of your enemy country?

Who is it ruled by?

How distant are they? (Not just physically, but perceptually as well.)

Topography

 What is the general topography?
Is it full of hills?
Is it full of trees?
(The presence of desert or forest will change the hardships available.)

How far is the nearest shelter? (non-city. By this I mean ruins, caves, forests, any place your character can or would run for safety.)

The nearest fresh water? (is it named?) **Named rivers, lakes and streams should always be included, spell them and give yourself Phoenetics.**

How far to the ocean? (if it is named, give that too.)

Are there any places that are uninhabited/uninhabitable?

If so, how far away? (You never know when places like this will come in handy for a chase scene.)

Mark and name any that apply.
Are we on:

An Island?

Mainland?

What is the nearest sea?

What is the nearest river? (potable?)

If you went two days inland, where would you be? (Generally, on any mainland, further from the sea.)

Where are we in relation to the Capital city?

If you went two days in each ordinal direction where would you be?

For seafarers:

Twenty days to sea?   Where are we?
****
For all:
When we start the story/ novel we are in (city)

Do we have neighbors?
 Are we in a large city?
 Small hamlet?
 Barony?
 Fifedom?
Metropolis?

meteorological data:

What time of year are we in?

What is the weather like?
  Rainy?
Wet?
Cold?
Dry?

MISC
  Are there natural disasters such as (but not limited to)
Are there rains of fire from meteor storms?
Are there deluges every year?
What precautions do travelers need to take?

A lot of these seem like useless questions, but if your MC and his or her merry band end up outside the city for any length of time, or we need to know why it is important that they NOT leave the city, it is information you need to have on hand.

Would they be likely to meet other travelers?
  If so would they be the same race/religion/creed/language of the MC and his/her group?

If not, why not?

How would that affect their reaction to the travelers?

Would there be any places inside or outside the city that would be either safe or taboo for any of the MC's crew?

  If so, name and explain.

How would they react if they could/not reach that place for some reason?

Is there a major landmark?
Within the city?

Without?

If so, is it:
man made?

Natural?

How far is it from where the MC starts his/her journey?

Is it always visible?

Is there any reason that the MC or their crew would need to go to or avoid said landmark, if so, how can you disrupt that?

Era

What is the general age? (old civilization or new?)

What is the general time period?

Is there magic? (you remember that separate piece of paper, this would be a good time to write down a little about the magic system.)

What is the most common method of travel?

Does it vary by class?

 What is the average speed of travel?

How far is it to the edge of the known world? (mi/KM or other measure)

 How long?

 (How much time, given the type of travel would it take to get there? Is there anything that would make that longer or shorter?)

Is there any place they would routinely avoid for some reason other that geographic or environmental factors?

 (a holy or unholy place? A graveyard? Something else?)

Perceptual world

How "big" is the world to a native? (In other words how far is it to unexplored lands?)

How 'long is it from 'end to end'? (perception only)

How far from the end of the world does your MC live/work? (KM/Mi and perception)

Perceptual world negations

Is there something magical or technological that routinely negates the distance of travel? If so:

Is it available to everyone?
If not:
who has access?

Who does not?

What are the limitations of this negation?

What is the political world view?

Are the neighboring cities/states/countries friendly or hostile?

What is the basis of the discontent (political, socio-economic, religious etc...)

What type of society is your MC from?

His/her neighbors?

During the course of the story will your MC be working within or without that society? (a fight for class justice? Freedom? Etc.)

Does their class, government, religion or anything else affect their world view?

In fifty words or less what is your MC's world view?
(don't worry if you can't answer these, that is what sections one through seven are for.)

****

Assignment, Complete at least three of the following assignments.

Foundations 1A

You are writing an Almanac entry for special dates in your city/state/people's history, or a date or dates that are important to your story.

Foundations 1B

You are writing propaganda for the area's biggest paper, why should people come to your area to vacation?

Foundation 1C

You are writing propaganda for a neighboring city/state, why should people NOT travel there?

Foundations 1D

Answer the foundations 1C propaganda. Paint a vivid picture that is different than the propaganda picture provided

Section two:
OOheeeOooahah… Or, call the mage.

If you checked the "use magic" Section then you need to park here a while. Here are some things you need to note down. (This section is also for those of you who have those with Psychic/Psionic abilities.)

Magic Type:(Casting vs scry) etc....
(for abilities, passive VS active)

How do they mark or activate the magic? (Or abilities?)

How are magic users garbed? (Are those with abilities marked in any way)

Do magick users use Technology? (Psychics?)

  Is there any technology they CANNOT use?

  Is there any tech that ONLY they can use?

What type of magic do they use?
Can they summon the summer winds? Do they control the waters? Can they call fire?

Or is it mind reading, fortune telling and scrying? What is the basic magic type? (For the sci-fi types, this is what you check with any sort of powers like telepathy, telekinesis. They run by the same rules.)

What is the cost of their 'magic' or ability? Does something have to be given (like alchemy?) or is it a physical toll? How 'big' can their abilities get? How small?

For Psychics, what is the cost for them, how long does it take to recover.

What are the practitioners called? Are they aligned good or bad?

How do others feel about them?

 Are they part of a religious system?

Are they against the religious system?

Neutral?

Are there sacred places?

Are there taboos for practitioners of certain types of magic? (Or abilities)

How would you know a magic user? What is their garbing like? Do they have anything specific that they ALL carry or do? Do they dress a certain way? Do they paint, pierce or tattoo themselves?

If they are not religious, then how does the religious class react to them? The government? The commoners?

Assignment 2:

Your friend needs a mage/magic user/psychic. In a scene using vivid detail describe why they would need a magic user (Psychic, what have you) and how they would contact or recognize one? Why would they need the magic user? How would they pay for the services? Would the neighbors know? Would they travel long distances to find them? Are there particular things they must do? Particular things they must not do? Are there consequences for calling a magic user/mage/psychic? What are they? Why?

When? Or, From here I can see the world.

General time period:

(General time period is ERA not date.)

 What is your era's tech?

(Does your world/city have something unexpected for the era?)

Is there magic?

If so how does magic and technology intersect?

Is there any technology that is out of place or that might SEEM to be magic?

When we are is almost as important as where we are. When is going to tell us what the general technology level of our world is, and thereby the size of our perceived world. Perceived world is the edge of the 'known world' the comfort level. The point at which you run into the 'here there be dragons.'

People can only perceive so far beyond their immediate area. For someone who doesn't travel by anything but horse, the perceived world might be the eastern seaboard, or the Virginia Territory. It is the point at which, to them, the world ends. The places they cannot go because of distance, language or world-view can also affect this.

In the days of Columbus and before, the seafarers believed that there was nothing outside of Europe "here there be dragons' it was the end of the known world.

 Are there unexplored areas on your civilization map?

Now is the time to fill them in, even if they never get used you need to know about them, because those places, and the stories they generate are part of the cultural identity, and psyche of the people. If your people live at the 'edge of the world' they are going to have a considerably different world view than those who are days, weeks or months away.

Perceived world view also takes into account the method of travel. For instance, a horse can only go so far in a given day. This is the time to do your research. This is the time to figure out how far logistically speaking, your quest will take you and if it is realistic to have it happen over a week, or over a year.

What sort of technology do they have?

Are they pre steam? Pre-Gunpowder? Post flight? Post nuclear? Pre-history? A general time period gives you a good idea of the rules.

Are any types of technology forbidden?

If so:

Why?

Are any places within the perceived world forbidden?

If so:

Why?

How far away from where your Quest starts does it end?

Assuming that nothing went wrong, and all of the trip was without incident, how long should the trip take?

Where does your MC live in relation to the start and end of the Quest?

What about your Antagonist?

If there are forbidden places mark them on the map, and mark them for what they are, not for what the people know.

Is there anything available that bends the rules of travel? If so, now is the time to add that card to the deck.

Assignment 3:

Perceptual world.

      Your main character is planning for the journey. Have him tell you, in detail the things he knows about the place he is going. Have him also tell you the things he is afraid of. Free write a scene in which your character is telling you about the journey your story is about to take him on. Have your MC tell you how long, how far, and how much they will need to pack, what the terrain is like, and why they are afraid to go. Is this a trip they have taken before? Do they know the route? Have them talk directly to You the writer.

Foundations: 4

Hail to the chief? Or is Service mandatory?

Government affects a lot of the culture. A Classed, oppressive, socialist society will react differently than a classless hunter-gatherer society.

Society type: (Classed? Classless? Some variation of?)

Does using Magic affect the class? What about religous affiliaton? Education? What are the class separations? Are there any exceptions?

Is there a working class? A nobility? Any special classes?

What sort of government is it? A dictatorship? A monarchy? A theocracy? Why? Do they have any 'strange' needs in that particular kind of government? How do they deal with police? Military? Can people get a fair trial? Do they even use courts?

Money:

Is there a standard currency? If so, what is it called? How much is it? What is the smallest denomination? The largest? What does it look like? (Paper or coin.)

Give a short list of equivalencies. (IE.

.01 "penny"

.10 "Dime".... etc

What type of market is it? Is it free market? Is it socialist? Do they not use money at all? Is it a debt and favor system? Is there a standard currency? If so, what is it called? How is it measured? What is average wage? For the poor? For the Rich?

What are the social classes? Is it a classed society? Is it classless? Who are the highest class? The lowest? What sort of social services/responsibilities are expected of each? How are the classes split? Money? Race? Language? Heritage? Job?

Do they have any freedoms? Do they expect any? How does the government deal with Rogues and dissidents? Is theft a problem? Is the government benevolent? Corrupt?

Where in the social ladder does your Main Character fall? Why? What is expected of him or her? What is taboo? Why? Are there places they cannot go? Places they should not go? Will his or her journey force them to go against that norm? How? In what way, and what punishment can they be expecting. (This plays in directly to the reader's question: What is at stake?)

Law and government:

How is the law handled? What is their highest authority? Do they believe in capital punishment? How do they deal with magic and the law? How does their religion play into or go against their government?

Is there a legal system? How is it characterized? Is it "Fronteir law" Full of vigilante justice? or is a 'big brother' sort of lockdown regime? Is it lax? harsh?

Is it safe for her to go out at night? Is he likely to get arrested for race, religous affiliation, magic use? Is theft a crime? Can you speak freely?

What type of punishment is there?

Habitation and land:

Who can own land?

Who cannot?

Foundations Section Four:

Your friend has run afoul of the government. In a detailed scene using vivid imagery and dialogue, have your friend describe what happened. Discuss the consequences of the crime, and what the legal options are right now. Focus on imagery and detail. Where will they be held? What sort of punishment are they in for? How soon? Are they to be tried? Is there even a right to a trial? Does their class affect the way they are judged? How?

Foundation: 5

Braaaains! Or School's out forever?

The next question to ask is about the education of the masses. Is there a state sponsored education program? What does education consist of? Anything we would not expect? Are there restrictions on who may go to school? If so, what are they?

Are there restrictions on what may or may not be taught? If so, what are they and why? Are there certain things that only some classes can learn? Is reading and writing part of the schooling? Is it the same for everyone? What language is schooling conducted in?

How often do they go to school? When do they start? How many days a week? What ages? What are the primary subjects?

If there is a written language, how is it written? (alphabetic? Runic? Heiroglyphic? Is everyone allowed to read and write? Are any classes Illiterate?

Does magic use or religous affiliation (or lack thereof) affect the education system. Can you choose what you take in school or does the government tell you what job you will have and therefore what classes you will take?

Are non natives allowed in school? Visitors? How do they view mixed race/mixed class students?

What is your MC's schooling? Is it typical for his/her class? Is it atypical? Can he write? Can she read?

Foundations assignment 5: education

Your friend is moving to your MC city, and they have children. In a scene using description and vivid detail have them compare and contrast the education from our world to the new one. Don't forget such topics as educational taboos and class differentiation.

Or

Your friend is moving to the MC city, have your MC tell them what education they can expect for their children. Again, use vivid detail and description.

Its greek to me.

What is your world/town's primary language? Who is it spoken by?

What is the secondary language? Whom is it spoken by?

Are there any dialects? Idialect? How are the languages and dialects divided?

Are they segregated by race, culture, creed, job? Something else?

Do they use the same colloquial language for ceremonies and religious observances?

Or is there another language for that?

Is your language decided by status?

Does magic affect your language?

What language does your MC speak? Why?

Assignment Six

Your friend is running into the language barrier. Give them a crash course in how not to offend the locals. Focus on simple things they should and should not say. Focus also on any local idialects or accents needed. Remember, this is an Idiots guide. Be concise.

Foundations: 7

Bringing it all together.

Now is the time to flesh out the information that you have gathered, stop and look over your notes this far. See if there is still anything you need to stop and answer. Its ok to have some really general stuff right now, we will deal with that later after we hit the signal systems.

Assignment seven:

Go through and write a one to two page scene in which a traveler from our land gets caught in your world, focus on as many of the questions that were asked as you can. Again, this should not be an info dump, the idea is to describe it in a scene.

Signal Systems

Signal systems:
Overview

There are twelve signal systems. They are:

1.   Verbal
2.   Written
3.   Numeric
4.   Pictoral
5.   Artifactual
6.   Audio
7.   Kinesic
8.   Optical
9.   Tactile
10. Temporal
11. Spatial
12. Olfactory

Thinking about Signal Systems

   The easiest way to explain them is to have you think back. If you have ever been away from home for a long period of time when you came back, you noticed things that you hadn't noticed when you were last here. And I don't just mean the weeds under the porch. You notice the distance (or closeness) of things, and the colors, and the level and type of noise. All of these are things that are culturally ingrained into us. By going into another culture for a while we reprogrammed our signal systems and so when we come back there is a bit of 'culture shock.'

   For instance, some language learners, once they have learned (or been forced to speak another language for a long time) they find it hard to pronounce things the same way they used to in their own language. This is especially true of those who are multi-lingual. It is that first Signal systems telling them that something isn't 'normal.'

   Smell is also a signal system, but it plays into so many others. For instance, your sense of smell can evoke a cultural image. Certain cents are classified as 'holiday' and they are culturally accepted as being used that time of year. If you light a 'yule' candle the rest of the year, most people would think you were crazy.

1. Verbal

Speech is perhaps the best known signal system, and most often maligned. The "language barrier' is actually the signal system. The 'verbal' signal system is not just 'speech' that being language, like 'English' but also any sort of vocal utterance whether prayer, song, exclamation, profanity, vulgarity, or anything else.

Besides just the language itself, (English) Verbal has to do with the mood, and tone as well. So not just the language, but 'formal' or 'informal'. This is the difference between a verbal system of 'sir's and Madam's or one laced with Profanity. This is the difference between Tonal, and Atonal. Not just WHAT language, but how is it used?

Does it change depending on the speaker's status? The status of the one being spoken to?

Does it change with job?

With ability or title?

Are some more well spoken?

Are there dialects? Idialects? (Idialect, subtle changes in speech not reflected in the written word. A mid-western accent is an Idialect, from Idiom.)

Are there particular Regions or language groups that are dialectic? (English versus American English) if so, why?
What caused the language to split? What keeps them split?

What non-language verbal utterances do they use?

What are their songs like? (not instrumentation, but vocally.)

Signal Systems:
Assignment 1

Verbal:

Go back to the Language Exercise in Foundations, have your MC talk to two or three
different language groups, focus on what they say, how they say it, and any non-language
vocal utterances. What do they say when they are surprised? How do they exclaim in
fear? What are their songs like?

Writing: A system of signs or images used to convey meaning.

Written: Not the spoken language, but how it is written down. Again, not just what the language is "English", but also, how it is used.

  For instance, does everyone use it?

  Is it used differently for some jobs versus others?

  Is it used differently by other social Status?

Are there some people not Allowed to read or write?

What about 'racial' differences?

Does it relate to the spoken word?

If it is non-aphabetic what is it?

Is it Runic?

Is it alphabetic?

Is it Heiroglyphic?

This also plays into your education foundation.

Can your MC, and his or her crew read and write?

Can your antagonist read and write?

Signal System
Assignment 2

Written;

You are the 'scribe' or law clerk for your area. They have just passed a law codifying the written language as the only one for legal documents. In one to two pages, give us a quick overview of the written language and how it is used pursuant to this new law. A language table may be included if you have it. If not, give us the most common written words and spellings, the spelling(s) of the city, state town, the name of the language.

Signal Systems:
3   Numeric

Numeric: Use of signs, markers or gestures to quantify amount weight, distance, length or measurement.

What is your numeric base? (America uses a modified base ten.)

Why do they use the specific base? (is it say, a base five because they count on their hands?

Is it a base seven because it is a holy number?

How is it shown?

What is the most common way of tallying large numbers?

 If they have to show or tell numbers how would they do it?

Is there a specific sequence to numbering?

 Is it larger groups first? (Twenty and four?)

Or single numbers first (Four and twenty?)

Do they use specific words?

What are the values of those words?

Signal systems:
Numeric

Assignment 3

You are a trader who is new to the area. This is your first time in the city and they are asking you to fill out a bill of lading. You are having trouble with their number system until you figure out their base. Explain to one of the other new traders what their number system is, and how to fill out the bill of lading that allows you to tally your load.

Signal Systems:
4. Pictoral

Pictoral: Signs, emblems and symbols assigned meaning beyond their physical appearance. Pictures, signs and emblems used to evoke the same thought or feeling in all, or to give tangibility to an intangible.

Our Pictoral system is vast and spans the gamut from "lady Liberty" to "blind Justice" to "Cupid" and "uncle sam."

 Each of these, to us has a specific meaning and image.

 Saying just the name evokes a specific image or feeling. This is the pictoral Signal system.

It deals with cultural Icons, deity, demigods, Ideals, abstracts. Pictoral images are often found on houses of worship, and places of the dead.

Unsurprisingly Death and afterlife have spawned more pictoral cultural ideals Than any other subject.

How are places of worship marked?

Places of death?

Do they use images for deities? For demigods? For Ideals? For abstracts?

Signal Systems:
Assignment 4

Pictoral
You have walked into a culturally significant building or place, (seat of government, graveyard, religious place,) In 1000 words describe the building, focus on the pictoral elements of design, the figures, emblems and signs that are prevalent and why they would be there. What do the images mean to those who enter? To those who pass by?

Artifact: An object with cultural significance, held in some esteem whether good or evil, used in a specific way.

Artifact covers a lot of society.

This includes everything from clothes to utensils.

For those in the sci-fi areas, don't forget technology. Think of what an archaeologist would be most likely to dig up.

Where would they find it?

How would it be used?

Why that specific way?

Why that specific place.

This is also the clothing they wear, the jewelry, the tools they use, the hair clips, the makeup they use, the toys their children play with.

Assignment 5

You are an Archaeologist from the future studying this long-dead culture. What have you found? Where did you find it? How was it used? Focus on the Physical objects not the decoration (pictoral) on them. Do you find certain objects at particular places, and only there? Why would that be? Does that change how the object is used?

Audio:
Sounds, other than language used to communicate thoughts and emotions of collective or cultural signifcance.

This is all the other sound, things like music, air raid sirens, thunder.

  Whatever non-verbal sounds have cultural meaning.

How do people react to specific sounds, or lack of them.

Is there a sound the associate with death?
With life?
With good?
With evil?

Sound is used in every day life. What sounds mean danger? What sounds mean safety?

Do they revere some bird calls over others? Do they fear thunder, or the rattle of the Snake?

  How is sound used in their every day life?
Is it permissible to shout?
Is it polite to belch?

Signal Systems
Assignment 6

Audio

You are visiting your MC world/ city/ village and hear a strange sound. When you get the attention of the locals and tell them of the sound, how do they react? Why? Have them explain what the sound is, and what it means to them. Should you fear it? Why? Why not?

Optical: The use of light and color to convey cultural significance and meaning.

Optical is one of the most prevalent of the signal systems. It isn't just light and dark but also colors. Here in America, you wear white to a wedding and black to a funeral, in some other countries that is reversed.

We all have colors that are 'safe' to us. (think green light) or danger (yellow, red) we have colors of pride (blue) and many others. How a culture uses light, dark and color can be significant. If red is a bad color to a culture, you would not wear a red t-shirt to a wedding, though possibly to a funeral.

What colors are neutral? Safe? Danger?

Are there any colors your MC would not wear? Why not?
Are there any superstions related to color?

Optical

You are going to be staying in your MC's city, town or province. He or she must quickly tell you about what colors to stay away from and what colors are safe. What are the associations with certain colors? Are some items more or less holy if they are another color? What colors are Taboo? Why?

Kinesic: Movement, specifically body language, position or habitual signs.

Kinesic deals with movement and space.
  Not touch, but movement. What movements do they make when they are afraid?

  Do they cross themselves?
What gestures do they use when they speak? Why?

Can some words just not be said because of taboo and so they sign them?
What gestures do they use when they are angry?
Happy?
Which gestures are vulgar?
Protective?

Kinesic.

Your mc has been struck dumb by a spell or by technology (Depending on if it is sci-fi or fantasy) he or she is unable to write, (perhaps doesn't know, perhaps forbidden) without dialogue, using signals and body language figure out who is telling the truth and who is lying to you. Figure out how to get to the one person who can help you restore your speech.

Touch.
In every culture touch means something different. Tactile refers to touching people and things. Is holding hands permissible? Is there an artifact or building they always touch when they pass? Is there something that they are forbidden to touch? What tactile sensations are 'safe' (Does homespun feel better to them than silk because one is familiar and the other not?)

How large is personal space? How do friends touch? Lovers? Families? Do they kiss on the cheek (one or both)? Or do they clasp forearms?

Tactile

You are busy getting yourself in trouble. You have unwittingly intruded on personal space and/or made a gesture or touch that is inappropriate or rude. Have your MC explain to you what you have done wrong and how to fix it. Remember, you are dealing with touch and space. So you might inadvertently flip someone off, but we are more concerned with touching the arm of a woman who is not your wife… etc.

Temporal: Judgment and marking of time. This includes not only the standard nomenclature of the day (how long is one 'day' etc) but also the meaning and weight of time in their culture. By this we mean, in some cultures it is polite to be a little late so as not to seem too eager. Some cultures it is considered rude to be late. For example, in Indonesia, using 'rubber time,' if you say the meeting is at ten, as long as it starts by 10:59:59 you are not late.

What is their view on time? Is it polite to be early? Is it polite to be late? When are the festivals or observances, why are they when they are?

Temporal

You have been invited to a state occasion, party or meeting in your MC's city. He or she is advising you on timing. In a detailed scene of dialogue have your character coach you in proper timing and what it means to be early or late. When does the meeting or dinner start? What time should you be there? If it is an 'odd' time, have your character explain the meaning.

Spatial-relationships of space and placement.

Spatial overlaps just a bit with tactile since it also involves personal space. This is more relationships between things. In America, doors are usually to the right of heavy traffic, up escalators are to the right of the down usually, and big deals in stores are set just right of center. All of these have to do with Spatial relationships. Since most people are right-handed we have developed a 'right-handed' culture. Handheld things are often ergonomic for the right hand.

Spatial also refers to the placement or segregation of our life. Generally things and places are used for one thing, and only one thing. In some cultures it is bad to have a kitchen and a seating area together.

In some places it is good.
Those are both spatial relationships.

Certain buildings are always found in certain places, and are generally made in certain shapes.

Is your character used to any spatial relationships that are unusual from our point of view?

Spatial

You are wandering around in your MC city. Explain their use of space and dimension.
Are some buildings built larger than others because of power, prestige or status? Are
some buildings always built to the right or left of another? How do they use personal
space, do they reach to shake your right hand? Or clasp your left forearm? How do they
use space and what is their dominant spatial orientation? Do people tend to move right?
Left? Do they expect others to move? How long is personal space?

Signal systems
12   olfactory

How does a culture use smell? What things are pleasant? Unpleasant? What smells are associated with which things. Here in America saffron is a cooking spice, but in some countries it is used for the dead. The meaning of the smell changes from culture to culture.

Signal Systems
Pulling it together

Signal systems are not used individually. Instead, they tend to be used many at a time, sometimes all twelve at once, sometimes three or four. But they always show up. Go back through the twelve assignments and look them over. Go back and make sure that you have filled in your foundations and your signal systems.

Signal Systems
Assignment 13

In a scene using vivid detail and dialogue, show at least eight of the twelve signal systems for your character's world. The scene may be as long or as short as you want, but you must work in at least eight of the signal systems. Don't call attention to them, just put in the smells, the feels, the sounds, put in what the system is to them, don't mention them directly.

Ok, now that you have the signal systems, it is time to start making some decisions.

Firstly, fill out the Norms/taboos sheet at the bottom of the page. This is going to help you decide what particular signal systems are going to affect your character and his/her life in your story.

Norms are your expected behaviors, things you should do, reactions you should have.

Taboos are things you should NOT do. This is your cultural thou-shalt and thou-shalt not list for this new people, and this list is going to show you some of their unconscious reactions to certain things.

Fact Check:

Stop and look back. Do your norms and taboos/ signal systems change any of your Cultural Foundation answers. If so, now is the time to change them.

Food for thought:

Does your character have norms/taboos that others of his/her race/culture would not, if so, note these and explain.

Do your norms and taboos fit your time and place?

If not, change something.

Does your government fit your norms and Taboos?

Do you have any taboo 'wildcards' things that cannot be catagorized? If so note and explain them.

	Norms	Taboos
1. Speech		
2. Written		
1. Numeric		
2. Pictoral		
3. Artifactual		
4. Audio		
5. Kinesics		
6. Optical		
7. Tactile		
8. Temporal		
9. Spatial		
10. Olfactory		

Bias

What are the cultural Bias' of your people? What people do they trust? Do they not trust? Why? Now is the time to write the history of the betrayal that made them hate their neighbors. Even if you don't use the information, you need to know it so that it can be worked into what the reader is reading.

World View:

Do the Signal systems/foundation and bias questions change the worldview any? If so, tighten it up now and get them all saying the same thing

Fact check:

Are you writing first person? Make sure your bias' and World View are clear or the reader will never trust/mistrust the narrator. If you are having trouble with lack of trust on the narrator, try checking your bias, maybe you did not explain something.

Are your language references correct? Do you have them speaking the right dialect? Do you have them in the right part of the government/society?

Strangers:

How do your people react to strangers? why? Are strangers/ travelers common? Welcome? Why/ why not?

Is there a particular place travelers might be coming from? Does this make a difference in their welcome? why? Why not?

Why are they traveling?

Travel And Logistics

Now it is time to think about your specific story.

How long is your quest? How much time does it span? How much ground does it cover? Given the travel limitations you set forth in "foundations" is that logical?

How long should a trip of that length be? How much time does it actually take? Why the difference?

How much food should they carry?

Fact check:

Along the way your characters will run into trouble, what SHOULD their reaction be? What is it actually? Why?

Will the journey force them to break norms/ taboos? If so, what will their reactions be? How will the be recieved by their own AFTER breaking them?

Can they carry enough food and water? Why? Why not? If they lose their supply how will they get more?

Reader's questions to the Author:

These are the most common problems with writing. The list is not exhaustive, so please feel free to name some I missed.

Question 1: Teacher, is this on the test?

Cause: Spending a large amount of word space (more than one or two lines) on a character or place that is not important. Remember, when you do more than a one-off your reader will want to know if it is on the test... if it actually shows up again. If the answer is no, then prune, you may have an info dump.

(see conworlding)

Question 2: Wheretheheckarewe?

Cause: Too sparse on the physical description. Try adding a touch more of place. Give us more of the visual and spatial systems if it is a place that shows up again. If it isn't a place that shows up again consider moving the action to another place.

(See conworlding, Info Dump)

Question 3: And your name is again?

Cause: not giving enough detail about a particular person. Or, possibly having too many names starting with the same syllable. Jen John, Joe and Johan.

For solutions see Conworlding

Question 4: Is he/she/it a genie?

Cause: Illogical explanation. It means that you have stretched the suspension too far. Work on pruning to make it more manageable. Happens most often when you don't give a plausible reason for a power, or when you have more happen than could physically or mentally be tolerated. (genie from Aladdin: You'd be amazed what you can live through)

(For solutions see Conworlding)

Question 5: Where did you come from?

Cause: A character who either was never mentioned or mentioned early and forgotten about shows up again at an opportune moment. Go back and add in another reference or two, or give him a small part in a scene to remind the reader.

Question 6: Who is the man behind the curtain? (also called "your plot hole is open.")

Cause: A plot hole big enough to drive a semi with a double trailer through. Or, in a mystery or suspense, a cheap trick that showcases the fact that this is all contrived. Double check your plot look for anything that isn't supposed to be there, tie up loose ends and dangling threads. Obvious logical fallacies can only be taken so far before they become funny and unbelievable.

Question 7: What does this mean?

Cause: Usually undefined 'alien' word or phrase. If a reader comes to a full stop because they don't understand a custom or a word, they are likely to put it down. This is a question that should be answered in short order.

(See Conworlding)

In-text
       Out-of-text

* Newbie -- A character who asks a question; the answer is conworlding. The character might be on a guided tour (questions implied), analyzing something unknown to him (provides his own answers), or a stranger to the area who must be educated about the situation by a native. Need not be the same character throughout a work (a Mary Jane).

* Brief Aside -- Non-narrative text, not advancing plot; if it's longer than brief, it's an info-dump (usually not good).

* Flashback -- Memory or spoken dialog.

* Incluing -- Casting vocabulary or ideas or imagery in such a way that the context itself explains the unknown. This is a broad technique with many approaches. A classic example is Heinlein's line, "The door dilated"; obviously, it's a futuristic high-tech door, not a panel swinging on hinges. Juxtaposing a new thing with known things of the same sort works well; e.g., "I took bread and cheese and a strange pink fruit; but the sausages, cubes of deep-fried ham, barbequed zulvic, and roasted vrin carcasses were not at all appetizing." A recent example from FSFW: no one got the reference to "people looked like they were survivors of Andersonville"; this phrasing might inclue us with all we need to know: "people looked like the nearly-starved survivors of the Andersonville POW camp."

* Epigraph -- Text (usually quotes) at the beginning of a chapter; e.g. Irulan's writings in Dune.

* Fictional Reference -- Consulted by characters in-story, a resource such as a handbook, encyclopedia, computer database, historical marker; e.g. "Handbook Of The Planets" in Vance's Ports Of Call & Lurulu or the "Encyclopedia Galactica" in Adams's Hitchhiker's Guide To The Galaxy series.

* Prologue -- Often an info-dump.

* Footnotes -- There when you need it, but optional to read (some people annoyed by them).

* Endnotes, appendices, glossary usually in the back; Dramatis Personae usually in the front.

* Map or other infographic.

* Timeline.

There's obviously some overlap between in-text and out-of-text. All of these techniques can be in-book; but, in the case of a series, placement and completeness becomes a concern. Most of these techniques could be out-of-book conworlding, such as an "Encyclopedia Of" or "Guide To"; they might be printed separately (completeness is a concern) or maintained online.

www.ingramcontent.com/pod-product-compliance
Lightning Source LLC
Chambersburg PA
CBHW081854280526

45789CB00007B/2701